Heart & Home's
Charming Paint and Decoupage Projects

Heart & Home's
Charming Paint and Decoupage Projects

Melissa Frances

Sterling Publishing Co., Inc. New York
A Sterling/Chapelle Book

Chapelle, Ltd.:
Jo Packham
Sara Toliver
Cindy Stoeckl

Editor: Melissa Maynard

Art Director: Karla Haberstich

Graphic Illustrator: Kim Taylor

Copy Editors: Marilyn Goff and Anne Bruns

Stylists: Connie Duran and Suzy Skadburg

Photographer: Kevin Dilley for Hazen Photography

Staff: Kelly Ashkettle, Areta Bingham, Donna Chambers,
Emily Frandsen, Lana Hall, Susan Jorgensen,
Jennifer Luman, Barbara Milburn, Lecia Monsen,
Linda Venditti, Desirée Wybrow

Book Design: Lauren Monchik

Frances, Melissa.
Heart & Home's charming paint & decoupage projects / Melissa Scheefer.
p. cm.
Includes index.
ISBN 1-4027-1553-6
1. Decoupage. 2. Acrylic painting. 3. House furnishings.
I. Heart & Home (Company) II. Title.
TT870.F697 2004
745.7'23--dc22
                        2004003330

10 9 8 7 6 5 4 3 2 1
Published by Sterling Publishing Co., Inc.
387 Park Avenue South, New York, NY 10016
©2004 by Melissa Frances
Distributed in Canada by Sterling Publishing
c/o Canadian Manda Group, One Atlantic Avenue, Suite 105
Toronto, Ontario, Canada M6K 3E7
Distributed in Great Britain by Chrysalis Books Group PLC,
The Chrysalis Building, Bramley Road, London W10 6SP, England
Distributed in Australia by Capricorn Link (Australia) Pty. Ltd.
P. O. Box 704, Windsor, NSW 2756, Australia
Printed and Bound in China
All Rights Reserved

Sterling ISBN 1-4027-1553-6

If you have any questions or comments, please contact:
Chapelle, Ltd., Inc., P.O. Box 9252, Ogden, UT 84409
(801) 621-2777 • (801) 621-2788 Fax
e-mail: chapelle@chapelleltd.com
web site: www.chapelleltd.com

Space would not permit the inclusion of every decorative item photographed for this book, nor could all of the designers be identified. Many of these items may be referred to on the Ruby & Begonia web site: www.rubyandbegonia.com or by calling (801) 334-7829.

The copy, photographs, instructions, illustrations, and designs in this volume are intended for the personal use of the reader and may be reproduced for that purpose only. Any other use, especially commercial use, is forbidden under law without the written permission of the copyright holder.

Every effort has been made to ensure that all information in this book is accurate. However, due to differing conditions, tools, and individual skills, the publisher cannot be responsible for any injuries, losses, and/or other damages which may result from the use of the information in this book.

This volume is meant to stimulate craft ideas. If readers are unfamiliar or not proficient in a skill necessary to attempt a project, we urge that they refer to an instructional book specifically addressing the required technique.

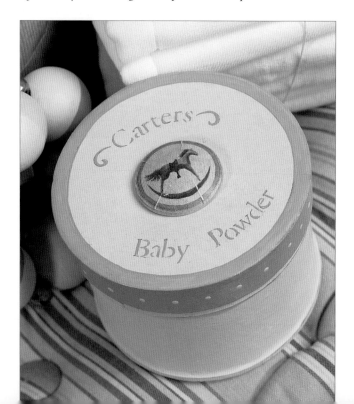

DEDICATION

I would like to dedicate this book to my parents Ed and Margie, whose love of antiques and history inspired me more than they will ever know.

And to Judy, whose talent and creativity never cease to amaze me.

— Melissa

Contents

INTRODUCTION

Melissa started Heart & Home in 1996 and the company has had a fast-pace growth ever since. Heart & Home is known for its nostalgic and exclusive designs. From cottage country to shabby chic, its products have been recognized for their authenticity and the ability to generate a heartwarming charm in any home.

One idea Melissa had to stay a step in front of the competition was to design her own style of antique labels with the help of her artist Judy Chaffey. The labels enabled Heart & Home to have their own look—unlike any other company in the industry. The labels are not reproductions but watercolor artwork, incorporated with a vintage design, to inspire a look that has never been seen before. With the success of their home products, they had thousands of inquiries from craft stores wanting to sell their labels. So in 2000, Heart & Home started marketing their peel-and-stick labels under the name Melissa Frances™. The response was incredible. Since then, crafters are finding new ways to enhance craft projects with Heart & Home's ever-increasing number of labels. During the process of making this book, they discovered that their labels are acid-free, opening a new chapter in Heart & Home's story. With their introduction into the scrapbooking industry, they are now developing new items for crafters to look forward to in the future.

INSIDE THIS BOOK

The Arts and Crafts industry has recognized what the Collectible industry has long known: that people have a deep-rooted desire for things that last—keepsakes they can create with their own hands and pass on to future generations. The projects in this book are designed with beginners and seasoned crafters in mind. Using both craft and decor products from Heart & Home, combined with wood, paint, and supplies (easily acquired at local craft stores) in addition to beautifully designed artwork labels from the Melissa Frances™ line, you too can create unique memories for generations to come. One last note: Don't be shy, marry your projects with genuine antiques to complete your vintage look. Try hanging your old dish rack on the wall to hold soap and tea towels. Many antiques can be used for different applications than what they were originally designed for. The photography in this book was designed to give you a variety of project and decorating ideas. However, a true crafter thinks "outside of the box" and is inspired by everything. They craft to make something unique to call their own.

A PRECIOUS VINTAGE-STYLE NURSERY

We all were young once! Some of us still are. I can never get enough of baby and small things. I collect all kinds of baby-related items, so this is my favorite section. This collection of projects is for the young at heart who love things too cute for words. You can craft these items for an adorable gift for a new mom or to decorate for the new baby or grandbaby.

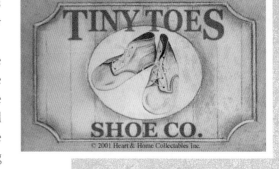

I am seeing a trend in decorating our babies rooms vintage. We are remembering the things we had when we were kids or the toys we could find at our grandparents' house. Usually in the basement where we were sent to play. If you study demographics like I do, you would be aware of the next baby boom coming. All of the baby-boomers are now becoming grandparents. These new grandparents are not moving out of the houses that they had their children in. Thus, they have a few extra rooms in the house after their kids moved out. So when they find out they are becoming grandparents, they are decorating their kids' rooms into nurseries. "Vintage nurseries" are the words for us nostalgic buffs.

A COZY ANTIQUE KITCHEN

What's hot? It's the kitchen! Don't just cook in it anymore, make it a room to remember. So much of today's decor is vintage and remembering Grandma's house. Some of our best memories at our Grandparents' house were the food they made and the time we spent in the kitchen. I believe another word for kitchen should be "family room."

In today's family rooms we just sit and watch television. There is not much talking to each other anymore. The television has deprived us of our communication time. But in the kitchen, it is another story: We cook, we talk, we laugh, and we even cry (I think it's the onions). Needless to say, the kitchen is where the heart of the family is. I am a firm believer in keeping televisions out of the kitchen.

While stirring the gravy, you can get one-on-one time with your children. Quality time can be enjoyed with other family members when they help with the meal. We are decorating kitchens to encourage people to come in and help. "Cute and Cozy" is the theme behind every vintage kitchen. This collection of projects can be used to decorate your kitchen or to give away as gifts for a special friend.

A WARM HEARTFELT CHRISTMAS

Decorate, decorate, decorate! We seem to never get enough of Christmas. It is the one time of the year that we decorating fanatics can get away with it. So many times my mom said to me that taking the time to make her a gift was so much nicer than buying her something. I truly believe her, and it was not just because I was eight years old. There is so much more thought that goes into making a gift for someone. In today's fast paced environment, we need to slow down and take the time to give thought to some of the little things in life. How much money I spend on someone should not be the deciding factor in gift giving. Take the time to show someone you care by making them something from your heart. The effort need not be the gift itself, it could be the packaging or you could scrap them a page of memories of past Christmases.

A CHARMING RETRO-STYLE LAUNDRY ROOM

The inspiration for designing a line of craft projects for the laundry came about from the idea that one can decorate any room—why not the laundry room! Many modern homes have the laundry room on the first or even the second floor. The laundry room can be a cute little hideaway room for those who either enjoy the tasks of doing laundry or not. Why not make it an environment that one can enjoy. Some of these projects can be used simply for decor or can be made as functional pieces to store odds and ends like that unmatched sock or button without a home. I prefer items that I can make myself and take pride in. Most of these projects look harder than they actually are. Don't be timid, get out of that laundry rut and create a room all your own.

A PRETTY FEMININE TOUCH

This category covers the vintage look for all avenues. Make a gift for a friend or make your own collectible to pass down through the generations. These projects will be sure to give every space in your house that vintage feel. Or they can start you on your own creative venture to think "outside of the box."

ABOUT THE LABELS

The labels that are featured in this book are from the unique Melissa Francis™ line of peel-and-stick labels. However, you may want to personalize your labels or select labels to coordinate with your style and decor.

To make your own labels, you can use photocopies of vintage photographs, pictures from books or magazines, or treasured children's artwork—the possibilities are endless. There are also many computer software programs available for creating labels. You can either print your labels on special paper that has a sticky side, or use one of the many decorative or textured papers on the market. The labels in this book may be photocopied for personal use only.

If you choose to print your labels onto nonadhesive paper, you will need to decoupage your labels onto your project. There are numerous decoupage products available, so choose the one that works best for your project. Decoupage medium comes in a variety of finishes—matte, gloss, waterproof, archival quality, tinted, etc.

Many of the projects call for sealer or stain. It is important that you avoid getting either of these on your labels for they may discolor and ruin your label. If you choose to apply the sealer under the sticker, make certain you wait until the sealer is completely dry before applying the labels or this may hinder the effectiveness of the glue you use.

Chapter One

A PRECIOUS VINTAGE-STYLE NURSERY

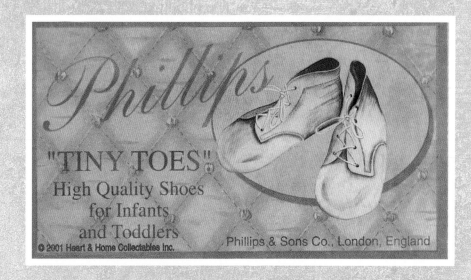

Phillips

"TINY TOES"
High Quality Shoes
for Infants
and Toddlers

© 2001 Heart & Home Collectables Inc.

Phillips & Sons Co., London, England

Est. 1896.

Carters

8 oz
Steralized

Baby
Powder

Ohio. U.S.A.

© 2001 Heart & Home Collectables Inc.

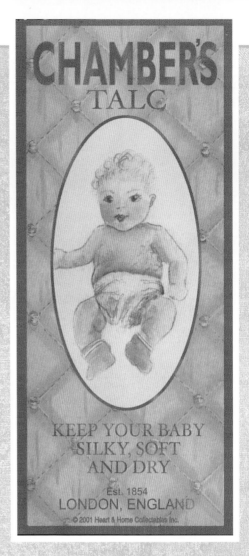

CHAMBER'S
TALC

KEEP YOUR BABY
SILKY, SOFT
AND DRY

Est. 1854
LONDON, ENGLAND

© 2001 Heart & Home Collectables Inc.

WARREN'S
Baby Accessories

© 2001 Heart & Home Collectables Inc.

A

© 2001 Heart & Home Collectables Inc.

Cotton
Tails

DIAPER SERVICE
Prompt & friendly service.

© 2002 Heart & Home Collectables Inc.

DECORATIVE BABY SHIRT

Materials

- *7¹/₂"x6" pressboard*
- *Vintage label*
- *Graphite paper*
- *Pencil*
- *Decorative Baby Shirt pattern on page 118*
- *Jigsaw or band saw*
- *Drill with ¹/₁₆" drill bit*
- *Fine sandpaper*
- *Damp cloth*
- *Acrylic paints, white and charcoal gray*
- *1" foam or flat brushes (2)*
- *¹/₄" angular or shader paintbrush*
- *Water-based stain*
- *Lint-free rag*
- *Acrylic sealer*
- *18-gauge wire (10")*
- *1"-wide sheer ribbon (6")*
- *Glue gun and clear glue sticks*

Step-by-Step Instructions

1. Using graphite paper and a pencil, transfer the Decorative Baby Shirt Pattern to the pressboard.
2. Carefully cut out pattern, using a jigsaw.
3. Drill two holes along the top of the shirt, approximately 2" apart.
4. Lightly sand outside edges and wipe clean with a damp cloth.
5. Using a 1" foam brush, apply two coats of white acrylic paint to the entire surface of the shirt. Allow to dry completely between coats.
6. Using angular paintbrush and charcoal gray acrylic paint, add shading around the edges, the neckline, and down the center of the shirt, creating two vertical lines and buttons.
7. For a weathered or worn look, lightly sand the outside edges. Wipe clean. For an aged look, apply a small amount of water-based stain to the entire project after sanding, using a lint-free rag.
8. Referring to the color photograph on the opposite page for placement of the label, apply the vintage label to the bottom-right corner of the shirt.
9. Optional: Personalize this piece by adding a name or birth announcement.
10. Using a 1" foam brush, apply a thin coat of acrylic sealer to protect and seal the presswood, except on the label. Let dry.
11. Create a wire hanger, using the 18-gauge wire and feeding it through predrilled holes to attach it to the shirt.
12. Tie the sheer ribbon into a bow and glue it to the top center of the shirt.

NURSERY ORGANIZER

Materials

- 8"x8"x4¼" wooden organizer
- Vintage label
- 1" foam or flat brushes (2)
- Acrylic paint, cream
- Fine sandpaper
- Water-based stain
- Lint-free rag
- Craft knife
- 9"x9"x⅛" balsa wood

Step-by-Step Instructions

1. Using a 1" foam brush, apply two coats of cream acrylic paint to the entire surface of the wooden box. Allow to dry completely between coats.
2. For a weathered or worn look, lightly sand the outside edges. Wipe clean. For an aged look, apply a small amount of water-based stain to the entire project after sanding, using a lint-free rag.
3. Adhere the vintage label to the front panel of the wooden box.
4. To make section dividers, use a craft knife to cut the balsa wood to the depth and height of the wooden organizer's interior.
5. Using a 1" foam brush, apply two coats of cream acrylic paint to both sides of the balsa wood pieces. Allow to dry completely between coats. Insert vertically into box.

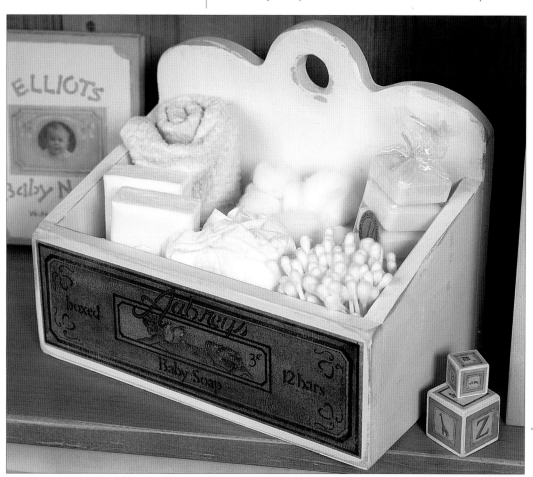

VINTAGE BABY BLOCKS

Materials

- *Wooden cube blocks*
- *Vintage labels (one for each side of a wooden cube block)*
- *1" foam or flat brushes (2)*
- *Acrylic paint, white*
- *Fine sandpaper*
- *Water-based stain*
- *Lint-free rag*
- *Acrylic sealer*

Step-by-Step Instructions

1. Using a 1" foam brush, apply two coats of white acrylic paint to all sides of the wooden cube block. Allow to dry completely between coats.
2. For a weathered or worn look, lightly sand the outside edges. Wipe clean. For an aged look, apply a small amount of water-based stain to the entire project after sanding, using a lint-free rag.
3. Referring to the above color photograph and working with one label at a time, adhere the vintage labels to the sides of the wooden cube block.
4. Using a 1" foam brush, apply a thin coat of acrylic sealer to all sides of the wooden block, except on the label. Let dry.

GIRAFFE BABY MUG

Materials

- *Papier-mâché baby mug*
- *Vintage label*
- *1" foam or flat brushes (2)*
- *Acrylic paint, cream*
- *Fine sandpaper*
- *Water-based stain*
- *Lint-free rag*
- *Acrylic sealer*

Step-by-Step Instructions

1. Using a 1" foam brush, apply two coats of cream acrylic paint to the outer and inner surfaces of the baby mug. Allow to dry completely between coats.
2. For a weathered or worn look, lightly sand the outside edges. Wipe clean. For an aged look, apply a small amount of water-based stain to the entire project after sanding, using a lint-free rag.
3. Optional: Personalize the mug by adding an individual's name.
4. Adhere the vintage label to the outer front center of the mug.
5. Using a 1" foam brush, apply a thin coat of acrylic sealer to the entire surface, except on the label. Let dry.

ASSORTED
HARD CANDY

Carnival

Family Favorite

FT. DODGE

IOWA
Est. 1852

Candy Treats

©2001 Heart & Home Collectables Inc.

CHECKERED
GIFT BAG

Materials

- *White craft or gift bag*
- *Vintage label*
- *1" stencil brush*
- *Acrylic paint, black*
- *Checkerboard stencils*

Step-by-Step Instructions

1. Using a dry 1" stencil brush and black acrylic paint, stencil the checkerboard patterns on the front of the craft bag.
2. Adhere the vintage label to the front of the craft bag.

Francis

ENAMELWARE
Est. 1862

Pieces to choose from are many, and include kitchenware as well as many essential bath products.

Francis

ENAMELWARE
Est. 1862

We offer a large selection of nostalgic enamelware, made of durable porcelain enamel.

Pieces to choose from are many, and include kitchenware as well as many essential bath products.

Flipper

Slippers

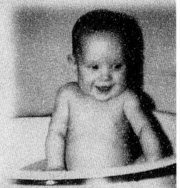

Francis
ENAMELWARE
Est. 1862

We offer a large selection of nostalgic enamelware, made of durable porcelain enamel.

Pieces to choose from are many, and include kitchenware as well as many essential bath products.

© 2002 Heart & Home Collectables Inc.

CREAM NURSERY STORAGE BOX

Materials

- *Wooden box with sliding lid*
- *Vintage label*
- *1" foam or flat brushes (2)*
- *Acrylic paint, cream*
- *Fine sandpaper*
- *Water-based stain*
- *Lint-free rag*
- *Acrylic sealer*

Step-by-Step Instructions

1. Using a 1" foam brush, apply two coats of cream acrylic paint to the entire surface of the wooden box. Allow to dry completely between coats.
2. For a weathered or worn look, lightly sand the outside edges. Wipe clean. For an aged look, apply a small amount of water-based stain to the entire project after sanding, using a lint-free rag.
3. Adhere vintage label to the sliding lid of the wooden box.
4. Using a 1" foam brush, apply a thin coat of acrylic sealer to the entire wooden box, except on the label. Let dry.

PAINTED
BABY GIFT PAILS

Materials

- Metal pails
- 1″ foam or flat brushes (2)
- Acrylic paints, assortment of colors including creams, blues, and browns
- Alphabet or number stencils
- Stencils of baby items
- Script paintbrush
- Pencil
- Acrylic sealer
- Gift items including stuffed animals, wooden blocks, or bath items

Step-by-Step Instructions

1. Using a 1″ foam brush, apply two coats of acrylic paint to the entire surface of a pail. Choose a color to complement your gift item. Allow to dry completely between coats.
2. With pencil and alphabet stencil, trace text around the top of the pail. Refer to the color photograph on the opposite page for text or create your own personalized message.
3. Optional: Instead of using a stencil, you may freehand the text or numbers.
4. Using a script paintbrush, fill in pencil marks with your choice of acrylic paint color. Let dry.
5. Paint nursery-related items onto the pail, using a stencil.
6. Optional: If you do not want to paint an image onto the pail, you may adhere a vintage label.
7. Using a 1″ foam brush, apply a thin coat of acrylic sealer to the painted surface of the pail.
8. Fill the painted pail with gift items.

© 2001 Heart & Home Collectables Inc.

CARTERS BABY POWDER TIN

Materials

- *Round tin with lid*
- *Vintage label*
- *1" foam or flat brush*
- *Acrylic paints, cream, camel, and pale blue-gray*
- *Circle template*
- *Pencil*
- *1/2" angular paintbrush*
- *Stylus*
- *Ruler*
- *Script paintbrush*
- *1 1/2" domed wooden disc*
- *Alphabet stencil*
- *Graphite paper*
- *Glue gun with clear glue sticks*

Step-by-Step Instructions

1. Using a 1" foam brush, apply three coats of cream acrylic paint to the tin, including the lid. Allow to dry completely between coats.
2. Using a circle template and pencil, mark a line on the lid, leaving a 1/2" border.
3. Using a 1/2" angular paintbrush, paint the border and side of the lid with three coats of camel acrylic paint. Allow to dry completely between coats.
4. Using a stylus, cream acrylic paint, and a ruler, mark equal dots around the side of the lid.
5. Using blue-gray acrylic paint and a script paintbrush, paint a fine line around the edge of the lid to separate the two colors.
6. Adhere vintage label to the domed disc.
7. Place disc on the center of lid and mark with pencil for future positioning. Set aside.
8. Using alphabet stencil and pencil, create the word "Carters Baby Powder" by tracing each letter onto a piece of paper the same size as the lid to form your words.
9. Optional: You may customize your own title.
10. When the layout of the letters is complete, transfer them onto your lid, using graphite paper.
11. Using script paintbrush, fill in letters with the blue-gray acrylic paint.
12. Glue disc on center of lid.

BABY ANNOUNCEMENT SCRAPBOOK PAGE

Materials

- Scrapbook page
- Vintage label
- Baby photographs
- Decorative paper
- $\frac{1}{2}$" sheer ribbon
- Pair of baby socks
- Letter beads to spell out the baby's name
- 24-gauge wire (two pieces: one long enough to hold beaded name; and one 5" for the rattle)
- $\frac{1}{2}$" flat paintbrush
- Acrylic paints, cream and either pink or blue, depending on the sex of the baby
- Half wooden bead
- Decorative cardstock
- Pieces of jewelry for photo corners
- Glue or adhesive tape

Step-by-Step Instructions

1. Create a name tag by handwriting the baby's name on decorative paper.
2. Optional: Use a computer to generate the text. Punch a hole on the left side of the tag.
3. Thread the sheer ribbon through the hole and tie a bow.
4. Optional: Include the baby's birth date and weight on the tag.
5. String the letter beads on the 24-gauge wire. Attach the wire to a pair of baby socks. Set aside.
6. Using $\frac{1}{2}$" flat paintbrush, paint the top portion of the half wooden bead with either blue or pink acrylic paint. Paint the bottom portion with cream acrylic paint. Let dry.
7. Fold a 5" piece of 24-gauge wire in half and twist to make the handle of the rattle. Glue to the back of the painted wooden bead to create the rattle.
8. Create picture frames with decorative cardstock to accommodate the baby photograph.
9. Arrange all pieces on your scrapbook page, including the vintage label. Be certain to attach all pieces securely to the page with either glue or adhesive tape.
10. Embellish the corners of the photograph with pieces of jewelry as a finishing touch.

BATH TIME SCRAPBOOK PAGE

Materials

- *Scrapbook page*
- *Vintage labels (3)*
- *Bath-related photograph*
- *Decorative paper*
- *Glue or double-sided tape*
- *Scissors*
- *Alphabet stickers or stencil*
- *Hole punch*
- *1/2" satin ribbon*
- *Cardstock*
- *1/4" angular paintbrush*
- *1/2" flat paintbrush*
- *Acrylic paints, white and gray*
- *Craft tag*

Step-by-Step Instructions

1. Place a photograph in the center of the scrapbook page.
2. Tear the decorative paper and adhere to the top-right and bottom-left corners of the scrapbook page.
3. Create Bath Time title by cutting out eight rounded-squares from cardstock. Punch a hole at the top of each square and thread the squares together with 1/2" ribbon. Adhere alphabet stickers to the front of each square.
4. Adhere the Bath Time title onto the scrapbook page. Layer pieces of decorative paper behind the title squares.
5. Cut out talc bottle shape from cardstock. Using 1/2" flat paintbrush, apply one coat of white acrylic paint to the cardstock. Shade the cap and edges of the bottle with 1/4" angular paintbrush and gray acrylic paint.
6. Optional: Add depth to the scrapbook page by attaching the bottle to the page with adhesive foam squares.
7. Thread a piece of 1/2" ribbon through the craft tag and adhere the tag to a piece of decorative paper. Place below the photograph.
8. Decorate the rest of the scrapbook page with vintage labels.

TOOTH FAIRY TREASURE BOX

Materials

- *Hinged wooden box*
- *Vintage label*
- *Ruler*
- *Pencil*
- *$\frac{1}{2}$" angular paintbrushes (2)*
- *Acrylic paints, including white, yellow, and mint green*
- *Fine sandpaper*
- *Water-based stain*
- *Lint-free rag*
- *$\frac{1}{2}$" flat paintbrushes (2)*
- *1" foam or flat brush*
- *Acrylic sealer*

Step-by-Step Instructions

1. Using a ruler and pencil, mark a rectangular shape on the top and sides of the box.
2. Referring to the color photograph on the opposite page and using a $\frac{1}{2}$" angular paintbrush, apply two coats of white acrylic paint to the marked rectangular shapes. Allow to dry completely between coats.
3. Using a $\frac{1}{2}$" angular paintbrush, apply two coats of mint green acrylic paint to the remaining areas of the box. Allow to dry completely between coats.
4. For a weathered or worn look, lightly sand the outside edges. Wipe clean. For an aged look, apply a small amount of water-based stain to the entire project after sanding, using a lint-free rag.
5. Adhere vintage label to the top of the box.
6. On each side of the box, using a ruler and pencil, draw a line for the wand.
7. Using a $\frac{1}{2}$" flat paintbrush, apply one coat of mint green acrylic paint to the drawn wand. Using a $\frac{1}{2}$" flat paintbrush, freehand a star on top of the wand with one coat of yellow acrylic paint.
8. Using a 1" foam brush, apply a thin coat of acrylic sealer to the entire surface of the box, except on the label.
9. Optional: Spray a light coat of spray sparkle over entire surface of box.

NURSERY STACKED STORAGE BOXES

Materials

- Set of three stacked papier-mâché boxes
- Vintage labels (3)
- 1" foam or flat brushes (2)
- Acrylic paints, white and seafoam green
- Stylus
- Fine sandpaper
- Water-based stain
- Lint-free rag
- Acrylic sealer

Step-by-Step Instructions

1. Using a 1" foam brush, apply two coats of white acrylic paint to the outer surface of each box, including the lid. Allow each coat to dry completely.
2. Using the stylus and seafoam green acrylic paint, add dots around each lid.
3. For a weathered or worn look, lightly sand the outside edges. Wipe clean. For an aged look, apply a small amount of water-based stain to the entire project after sanding, using a lint-free rag.
4. Adhere the vintage label to the front center of each box.
5. Using a 1" foam brush, apply a thin coat of acrylic sealer to each box and lid, except on the lid. Let dry.

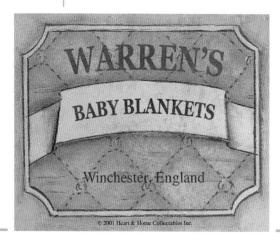

WARREN'S

BABY BLANKETS

Winchester, England

© 2001 Heart & Home Collectables Inc.

TEDDY BEAR BUCKET

Materials

- *Papier-mâché bucket with lid*
- *Vintage label*
- *Acrylic paint, cream*
- *1" foam or flat brush*
- *Fine sandpaper*
- *Soft clothes (3)*
- *Ruler*
- *Pencil*
- *Acrylic stain*
- *Teddy bear*

Step-by-Step Instructions

1. Using a 1" foam brush, apply three coats of cream acrylic paint to the papier-mâché bucket and lid. Allow to dry completely between coats.
2. Lightly sand the edges of the bucket and lid.
3. Remove excess dust from the surfaces with a soft cloth.
4. Using a ruler and pencil, measure and mark the center point of the front side of the bucket.
5. Adhere the vintage label to the marked center points. Smooth from the center to edges to remove any ripples.
6. Using a soft cloth, apply a light coat of stain to all of the painted areas on the bucket and lid to darken the distressed areas that you sanded off. Remove any excess stain, using a clean soft cloth.
7. After stain is completely dry, place the teddy bear inside the finished pail.

TEDDY BEAR CUPBOARD

Materials

- 2"x4"x5½" miniature wooden cupboard
- Vintage label
- Fine sandpaper
- 1" foam or flat brushes (2)
- Acrylic paint, khaki tan
- Water-based stain
- Lint-free rag
- Acrylic sealer
- Decorative accents including 3" teddy bears and miniature wooden blocks
- Glue gun with clear glue sticks

Step-by-Step Instructions

1. Lightly sand the entire surface of the miniature cupboard, removing any rough edges.
2. Using a 1" foam brush, apply two coats of khaki tan acrylic paint. Allow to dry completely between coats.
3. For a weathered or worn look, lightly sand the outside edges. Wipe clean. For an aged look, apply a small amount of water-based stain to the entire project after sanding, using a lint-free rag.
4. Adhere the vintage label to the center of the miniature cupboard door.
5. Using a 1" foam brush, apply a thin coat of acrylic sealer to the entire surface of the miniature cupboard, except on the label. Let dry.
6. Adhere the decorative accents.

BABY GIFT BUCKETS

Materials

- *Plaid metal buckets*
- *Vintage label*

Step-by-Step Instructions

1. Referring to the above color photograph, adhere a vintage label to the front of a plaid bucket.
2. Optional: As a quick shower gift, attach a Vintage Gift Tag as shown on the opposite page, to accent the Baby Gift Bucket.

VINTAGE GIFT TAG

Step-by-Step Instructions

1. To give the tag an aged look, dab a lint-free rag in stain and squeeze out excess so that rag is not saturated. Gently rub stain over tag before applying the label.
2. Optional: Stain can be rubbed over label to age the look of the label if desired; but this will darken the label considerably, and the effect cannot be reversed. An alternate distressing technique would be to use chalk. Rub chalk over tag alone, or tag and label, and wipe off any excess.
3. Adhere a vintage label to the tag.
4. Pull 8" piece of ribbon through the tag hole.
5. Simply tie off ribbon, or tie in a bow.

Materials

- *Craft tag*
- *Vintage label*
- *Water-based stain or brown-toned chalk*
- *Lint-free rag*
- *Sheer ribbon (8" per tag)*
  (Substitutes for ribbon can include rope, jute, regular cloth, patterned ribbon)

VINTAGE BABY DISPLAY CASE

Materials

- 2"-deep wooden display case
- Vintage label
- Vintage baby decorative accents
- Double-sided sticky Velcro

Step-by-Step Instructions

1. Remove the display backing from the wooden case.
2. Place the vintage label and the decorative accents on the backing. Once the placement is determined, apply double-sided sticky Velcro to the back side of the decorative accents and front of backing.
3. Optional: Personalize the display case by adding baby photographs or birth announcements.
4. Reattach the backing to the display case.

CHALKBOARD WINDOW FRAME

Materials

- Small wooden craft window frame
- Drill with ⅜" drill bit
- Fine sandpaper
- Acrylic paint, cream
- 1" foam or flat brushes (3)
- Water-based stain
- Lint-free rag
- Acrylic sealer
- Black chalkboard paint
- Chalk

Step-by-Step Instructions

1. Remove the backing from the frame and set aside.
2. Drill the desired number of holes into frame. The depth of each hole should be only ½".
3. Sand off any rough edges.
4. Using a 1" foam brush, apply two coats of cream acrylic paint to the entire surface of the frame. Allow to dry completely between coats.
5. For a weathered or worn look, lightly sand the outside edges. Wipe clean. For an aged look, apply a small amount of water-based stain to the entire project after sanding, using a lint-free rag.

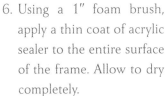

6. Using a 1" foam brush, apply a thin coat of acrylic sealer to the entire surface of the frame. Allow to dry completely.
7. Using a 1" foam brush, apply two coats of black chalkboard paint to the front side of the removable backing. Allow to dry completely between coats.
8. Reattach the backing and insert chalk into the holes.

BABY APPAREL STORAGE BOX

Materials

- *Wooden box with sliding lid*
- *Vintage label*
- *1" foam or flat brushes (2)*
- *Acrylic paint, cream*
- *Fine sandpaper*
- *Water-based stain*
- *Lint-free rag*
- *Acrylic sealer*

Step-by-Step Instructions

1. Using a 1" foam brush, apply two coats of cream acrylic paint to the entire surface of the wooden box. Allow to dry completely between coats.
2. For a weathered or worn look, lightly sand the outside edges. Wipe clean. For an aged look, apply a small amount of water-based stain to the entire project after sanding, using a lint-free rag.
3. Adhere the vintage label to the sliding lid of the wooden box.
4. Using a 1" foam brush, apply a thin coat of acrylic sealer to the entire wooden box, except on the label.

Chapter Two

A COZY ANTIQUE KITCHEN

Well's
ENAMEL
WARE
Est. 1867
Specializing in
Upscale European Design

© 2002 Heart & Home Collectables, Inc.

GRANNY'S
KITCHEN
BAKERY
As good as home-made!

© 2002 Heart & Home Collectables Inc.

SPENCER'S TEA

Entertain with the Finest

Net.
28 oz.   BOSTON, MASS.   12¢

CLASSIC BLEND

© 2001 Heart & Home Collectables Inc.

SUGAR MILL
1 lb.

15¢

Pure Cane Sugar

© 2001 Heart & Home Collectables Inc.

RICHMOND CO.

100% PURE
BAKING
SODA

12¢

100g.

© 2001 Heart & Home Collectables Inc.

GUARANTEED SATISFACTION

COUNTRY FAIR
JAMS &
JELLIES
Home Made Goodness!

© 2002 Heart & Home Collectables Inc.

GINGERBREAD MEN SCRAPBOOK PAGE

Materials

- *Scrapbook page*
- *Brown decorative paper, same size as scrapbook page*
- *Vintage labels (2)*
- *Gingerbread-related photographs*
- *Ruler*
- *Scissors*
- *White chalk*
- *Circle templates*
- *Craft knife*
- *White marker*
- *Cardstocks, brown and white*
- *1/2" sheer ribbon*
- *Sheet of vellum paper*
- *Glue or double-sided tape*

Step-by-Step Instructions

1. Cut brown decorative paper ¼" smaller than scrapbook page. Lightly apply white chalk over the brown paper to give the appearance of flour.
2. Using a circle template and craft knife, cut each photograph into a circle. Mount each photograph onto brown cardstock circles, cut slightly larger. Outline around the photograph with white marker. Set aside.
3. Cut out two gingerbread-men shapes from brown cardstock. Create the white outlines and facial features with white marker. With ½" ribbon, tie two small bows and attach them onto gingerbread men. Set aside.
4. Cut out bowl shape from white cardstock.
5. Optional: Cut out two gingerbread men from one vintage label and accessories with a wooden spoon cut out of brown cardstock. Set aside.
6. Either handwrite or computer-generate text onto the vellum paper. Refer to color photograph on the opposite page for text or create your own. Set aside.
7. Adhere all decorative pieces, including vintage labels, onto the scrapbook page.
8. Optional: Use adhesive foam squares to layer some decorative pieces on the page.

HARVEST KITCHEN PLAQUE

Materials

- *5"x 7" wooden plaque*
- *Vintage label*
- *3$\frac{1}{2}$"x $\frac{7}{8}$" wooden bucket handle*
- *Drill with $\frac{7}{32}$" drill bit*
- *Fine sandpaper*
- *1" foam or flat brushes (2)*
- *Acrylic paint, green*
- *Water-based stain*
- *Lint-free rag*
- *Craft knife*
- *Decorative foam apple*
- *Glue gun with clear glue sticks*
- *Needle-nosed pliers*
- *18-gauge wire (18")*
- *Acrylic sealer*

Step-by-Step Instructions

1. Drill holes in the plaque for handle, then lightly sand the wooden plaque. Wipe off any dust.
2. Using a 1" foam brush, apply two coats of green acrylic paint to the entire surface of the wooden plaque. Allow to dry completely between coats.
3. For a weathered or worn look, lightly sand the outside edges. Wipe clean. For an aged look, apply a small amount of water-based stain to the entire project after sanding, using a lint-free rag.
4. Adhere the vintage label to the front of the plaque.
5. Using a craft knife, cut the foam apple vertically in half. Using the glue gun, apply glue to the back side of one of the halves.
6. Referring to the color photograph on the opposite page, adhere over apple motif on the label.
7. Thread wooden handle onto 18-gauge wire, then feed wire ends through the predrilled holes from the back to front and secure by twisting the wire ends in a spiral, using needle-nosed pliers.
8. Using a 1" foam brush, apply one coat of acrylic sealer to the plaque edges, except on the label. Let dry.

WHITE KITCHEN CANISTERS

Materials

- *Set of three wooden canisters*
- *Vintage labels (3)*
- *1" foam or flat brushes (2)*
- *Acrylic paint, white*
- *Fine sandpaper*
- *Water-based stain*
- *Lint-free rag*
- *Acrylic sealer*

Step-by-Step Instructions

1. Using a 1" foam brush, apply two coats of white acrylic paint to the outer surface of each canister, including the lid. Allow each coat to dry completely.
2. For a weathered or worn look, lightly sand the outside edges. Wipe clean. For an aged look, apply a small amount of water-based stain to the entire project after sanding, using a lint-free rag.
3. Adhere the vintage label to the center of each canister.
4. Using a 1" foam brush, apply a thin coat of acrylic sealer to the exterior of each canister and lid, except on the label. Let dry.

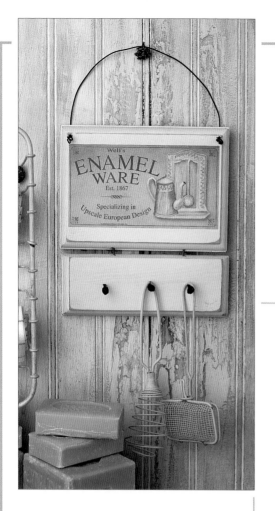

Materials

- *5" x 7" wooden plaques (2)*
- *Vintage label*
- *18-gauge wire (18")*
- *Drill with ³/₃₂" drill bit*
- *Power saw*
- *Hammer*
- *Decorative or vintage nails (3)*
- *Fine sandpaper*
- *Acrylic paint, white*
- *Water-based stain*
- *Lint-free rag*
- *1" foam or flat brush*
- *Acrylic sealer*

HANGING UTENSIL HOLDER

Step-by-Step Instructions

1. Drill holes in upper corners of the first wooden plaque to accommodate an 18-gauge wire hanger.
2. Center and drill two holes 2" apart on the bottom edge of the plaque to attach the smaller plaque.
3. Cut the second wooden plaque in half, using the power saw. Set one half aside.
4. Drill two holes on the top edge of the smaller plaque, aligning with the two holes on the bottom of the larger plaque.
5. Lightly sand edges on both plaques.
6. Using a 1" foam brush, apply two coats of white acrylic paint to both plaques. Allow to dry completely between coats.
7. Attach the two wooden plaques together by looping 18-gauge wire through the aligned predrilled holes.
8. Hammer the nails into the bottom plaques leaving enough room to hang the utensils.
9. For a weathered or worn look, lightly sand the outside edges. Wipe clean. For an aged look, apply a small amount of water-based stain to the entire project after sanding, using a lint-free rag.
10. Adhere label to center of the top plaque, smoothing out any ripples.
11. Using a 1" foam brush, apply acrylic sealer to both plaques, except on the label. Let dry.

WINDOW FRAME SHADOW BOX

Materials

- *22¹/₂"x17" wooden craft window frame*
- *Display items including vintage enamel dishes and kitchen utensils*
- *17"x1"x3" wood (2)*
- *22¹/₂"x1"x3" wood (2)*
- *1" foam or flat brushes (2)*
- *Acrylic paint, white*
- *Fine sandpaper*
- *Water-based stain*
- *Lint-free rag*
- *Acrylic sealer*
- *Drill or screwdriver*
- *1¹/₂" screws (8)*
- *Corner brackets (4)*
- *23¹/₂"x18" piece of toile fabric*
- *Roll of double-sided carpet tape*
- *Sticky Velcro tape to hold the display items*
- *Brackets to hold backboard in place (4)*

Step-by-Step Instructions

1. Remove the backing from the frame and set aside.
2. Using a 1" foam brush, apply two coats of white acrylic paint to the four 1"x3" wood pieces and to the frame. Allow to dry completely between coats.
3. For a weathered or worn look, lightly sand the outside edges. Wipe clean. For an aged look, apply a small amount of water-based stain to the entire project after sanding, using a lint-free rag.
4. Using a 1" foam brush, apply one coat of acrylic sealer to the frame edges. Let dry.
5. Using drill and screws, screw the four 1"x3" pieces together creating a square frame. Using corner brackets, attach the square frame to the window frame. This should extend the depth of the frame.
6. Measure and cut the toile fabric to fit smoothly on one side of the frame backing. Attach the double-sided tape to the backing and smooth out the fabric.
7. Using the sticky Velcro tape, attach the display items to the fabric backing.
8. Reattach the backing to the frame, using brackets and screws.

Chapter Three

A WARM HEARTFELT CHRISTMAS

© 2001 Heart & Home Collectables Inc.

LINDEN
TOY CO.

Family Owned and Operated

New York, N.Y.

WOODLAND DECORATING

Since 1921

"Trim your home with quality decorations"

© 2002 Heart & Home Collectables Inc.

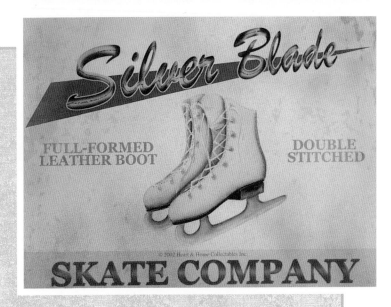

Silver Blade

FULL-FORMED
LEATHER BOOT

DOUBLE
STITCHED

© 2002 Heart & Home Collectables Inc.

SKATE COMPANY

DRUMMER
—BOY—

Quality Drums Since 1867

- Metal Sides
- Genuine Sheepskin
- Hardwood Drumsticks

© 2002 Heart & Home Collectables Inc.

LANTERN

Est.   1798

COMPANY

© 2002 Heart & Home Collectables Inc.

Yuletide
TREATS

Freshest
Ingredients

© 2002 Heart & Home Collectables Inc.

DECORATIVE SNOWMEN

Materials

- *7¾" papier-mâché posts (2)*
- *1" foam or flat brushes (2)*
- *Acrylic paints, white, black, and dark burgundy*
- *Acrylic sealer*
- *Graphite paper*
- *Pencil*
- *Decorative Snowmen Faces patterns #1 and #2 on page 119*
- *Stylus*
- *Sponge or stencil brush*
- *Ruler*
- *Decorative accents including cotton balls (3), 1" wooden discs (2), approx. 40" of remnant fabric or garland, infant sock, 24-gauge wire*

Step-by-Step Instructions

1. Using a 1" foam brush, apply two coats of white acrylic paint to the entire surface of both papier-mâché posts. Allow to dry completely between coats.
2. Using a 1" foam brush, apply a thin coat of acrylic sealer to both posts. Let dry.
3. Using the graphite paper and pencil, transfer the Decorative Snowman Faces patterns #1 and #2. With the stylus and the black acrylic paint, fill in the eyes, nose, and mouth of the snowmen. Add the rosy cheeks by applying a small amount of dark burgundy acrylic paint to a sponge and dab on lightly or in a swirling motion with a stencil brush.
4. Referring to the color photograph on the opposite page, use a ruler to create the lined border on the base of each post.
5. Optional: Instead of painting the lined edge, adhere a vintage label to the front of the posts for a more decorative touch.
6. Accessorize each post with the decorative accents.

SNOWMAN WINDOW FRAME

Materials

- *Small square craft window frame with Plexiglas*

- *1" foam or flat brushes (3)*

- *Acrylic paints, white (frame, snowmen), black (earmuffs), russet (nose, cheeks, hat, scarf), evergreen (scarf), charcoal gray (shading and highlight)*

- *Fine sandpaper*

- *Water-based stain*

- *Lint-free rag*

- *Acrylic sealer*

- *Snowmen Window Frame patterns #1–#4 on pages 120–124*

- *Transfer paper*

- *Pencil*

- *Paintbrushes assortment including flats, shading, and stencil*

- *Stylus*

- *Stencil brush or sponge*

Step-by-Step Instructions

1. Remove the Plexiglas from the frame and set aside.

2. Using a 1" foam brush, apply two coats of white acrylic paint to the frame. Allow to dry completely between coats.

3. For a weathered or worn look, lightly sand the outside edges. Wipe clean. For an aged look, apply a small amount of water-based stain to the entire project after sanding, using a lint-free rag.

4. Using a 1" foam brush, apply a thin coat of acrylic sealer to the frame. This will seal and protect the frame. Set aside.

5. Transfer Snowmen Window Frame patterns #1–#4 onto the front of the Plexiglas, using transfer paper and pencil. Refer to the Snowmen Window Frame Placement on page 120. Turn over to the back of the Plexiglas and fill in the snowmen forms with two to three coats white acrylic paint. Let dry.

6. Referring to the photograph on the opposite page and using the assorted paintbrushes and acrylic paints, paint the snowmen faces on the front of the Plexiglas.

7. Start with the earmuffs and earmuff wires. Next, base-coat the hats and the scarves.

8. Shade and highlight the snowmen, hats, and scarves.

9. Paint the eyes, mouths, and buttons.

10. Add the nose by using the stylus. Start at the base and with a very shaky hand, drag nose out to a point.

11. When the face is completely dry, use a stencil brush to apply color to cheeks.

12. Using a script brush, add white lines to the scarves and buttons.

13. Using a 1" foam brush, apply one coat of acrylic sealer over the entire project to seal and protect.

STAR CHRISTMAS TREE

Materials

- *Large flat papier-mâché stars (2)*
- *Medium flat papier-mâché stars (7)*
- *Small flat papier-mâché star*
- *3-dimensional papier-mâché star*
- *1" foam or flat brushes (3)*
- *Acrylic paints, green and white*
- *Fine sandpaper*
- *Water-based stain*
- *Lint-free rag*
- *Acrylic sealer*
- *Wooden dowel (7")*
- *Glue gun with clear glue*

Step-by-Step Instructions

1. Using a 1" foam brush, apply two coats of green acrylic paint to the entire surface of each flat papier-mâché star. Allow to dry completely between coats.
2. Using a 1" foam brush, apply two coats of white acrylic paint to the entire surface of the 3-dimensional papier-mâché star. Allow to dry completely between coats.
3. For a weathered or worn look, lightly sand the outside edges. Wipe clean. For an aged look, apply a small amount of water-based stain to the entire project after sanding, using a lint-free rag.
4. Using a 1" foam brush, apply acrylic sealer to each papier-mâché star. Let dry.
5. Insert the wooden dowel into the center of one large flat papier-mâché star. Secure with glue. Let dry.
6. Stack the remaining flat papier-mâché stars onto the dowel, creating a Christmas tree form.
7. Insert the dowel into the 3-dimensional papier-mâché star. Secure with glue.

HOLIDAY RIBBON BOX

Materials

- Wooden gift box
- Vintage label
- 1" foam or flat brush
- Acrylic paint, white
- Fine sandpaper
- Water-based stain
- Lint-free rag

Step-by-Step Instructions

1. Using a 1" foam brush, apply two coats of white acrylic paint to the wooden gift box. Allow to dry completely between coats.
2. For a weathered or worn look, lightly sand the outside edges. Wipe clean. For an aged look, apply a small amount of water-based stain to the entire project after sanding, using a lint-free rag.
3. Adhere the vintage label to the front of the wooden gift box.

TREE TOPPER COMPANY

HAND CRAFTED

FINEST QUALITY

© 2002 Heart & Home Collectibles Inc.

HOLIDAY Ribbon & Wrap

It's not just the gift that's Special!

Since 1817

© 2002 Heart & Home Collectibles Inc.

HOLIDAY BEARS

SINCE
1863

69¢
EACH

Finest

Qualite

DRUMMER
—BOY—

Quality Drums Since 1867

• Metal Sides
• Genuine Sheepskin
• Hardwood Drumsticks

HOLIDAY BEAR WOODEN FRAME

Materials

- *5"x 7" wooden frame*
- *Vintage label*
- *1" foam or flat brushes (2)*
- *Acrylic paint, white*
- *Fine sandpaper*
- *Water-based stain*
- *Lint-free rag*
- *Acrylic sealer*

Step-by-Step Instructions

1. Remove the backing from the frame and set aside.
2. Using a 1" foam brush, paint the frame with two coats of white acrylic paint. Allow to dry completely between coats.
3. For a weathered or worn look, lightly sand the outside edges. Wipe clean. For an aged look, apply a small amount of water-based stain to the entire project after sanding, using a lint-free rag.
4. Using a 1" foam brush, apply a thin coat of acrylic sealer to the wood frame. Let dry.
5. Adhere the vintage label to the front side of backing.
6. Reattach the backing to the frame.

PAPIER-MÂCHÉ HOLIDAY BOXES

Materials

- *Set of three papier-mâché gift boxes*
- *Vintage labels (3)*
- *$1/2$" foam or flat brush*
- *1" foam or flat brush*
- *Acrylic paint, dark red*
- *Fine sandpaper*
- *Water-based stain*
- *Lint-free rag*
- *Acrylic stain*

Step-by-Step Instructions

1. Using a $1/2$" foam brush, apply two coats of dark red acrylic paint to the outer surface of each papier-mâché box, including the lid. Allow each coat to dry completely.
2. For a weathered or worn look, lightly sand the outside edges. Wipe clean. For an aged look, apply a small amount of water-based stain to the entire project after sanding, using a lint-free rag.
3. Adhere the vintage label to the center of each box.
4. Using a 1" foam brush, apply a thin coat of acrylic sealer to the exterior of each papier-mâché box, except on the labels. Let dry.

© 2001 Heart & Home Collectables Inc.

CHRISTMAS SCRAPBOOK PAGE

Materials

- Scrapbook page
- Vintage labels (3)
- Cardstocks same size as scrapbook page, green corrugated and red
- Sheet of vellum paper
- Black textured paper
- Silver grommets (8)
- Black decorative tags
- Christmas photographs
- Evergreen tree charm

Step-by-Step Instructions

1. Adhere green corrugated cardstock to scrapbook page.
2. Measure 1″ in from each side of the red cardstock and cut out the center piece.
3. Cut the red center piece down to be 1″ smaller on all sides. Tear down the right side of the piece.
4. Tear off a section of the vellum paper and layer it underneath the red center piece.
5. Mount all vintage labels to a piece of black textured paper, cut ⅛″ larger than the label. Secure the mounted labels to the scrapbook page with grommets.
6. Prepare all mats for photographs by measuring vellum the size of each photograph and adding ⅛″. Cut the measured vellum and adhere photographs onto each piece.
7. Arrange and adhere matted photographs onto the scrapbook page.
8. Decorate the rest of the scrapbook page with the charm and decorative tags.

Chapter Four

A CHARMING RETRO-STYLE LAUNDRY ROOM

HUDSON

Est. 1869   American Made

WASHBOARDS

© 2001 Heart & Home Collectables Inc.

VINTAGE CLOTHES PEGS BOX

Materials

- 7¹/₂"x3¹/₄"x3¹/₄" wooden box
- Vintage labels (2)
- Fine sandpaper
- 1" foam or flat brushes (2)
- Acrylic paint, blue-gray
- Water-based stain
- Lint-free rag
- Hammer
- Decorative or vintage nails
- 18-gauge wire (30")
- Acrylic sealer

Step-by-Step Instructions

1. Lightly sand the entire surface of the wooden box, removing any rough edges. Clean off any excess dust.
2. Using a 1" foam brush, dry-brush blue-gray acrylic paint to the outer and inner surfaces of the wooden box. Let dry.
3. For a weathered or worn look, lightly sand the outside edges. Wipe clean. For an aged look, apply a small amount of water-based stain to the entire project after sanding, using a lint-free rag.
4. Adhere one label to each side of the wooden box.
5. Referring to the color photograph on the opposite page for positioning, hammer one decorative nail to each side of the wooden box.
6. Create a handle by wrapping each end of 18-gauge wire around the screws.
7. Using a 1" foam brush, apply a thin coat of acrylic sealer to the entire outer surface, except on the labels.

ELLMAN'S
WASHING MACHINES

SUPERIOR QUALITY

SINCE

1930

WESTFIELD, IN

© 2001 Heart & Home Collectables Inc.

DECORATIVE LAUNDRY BUCKET

Materials

- *Metal bucket with handle*
- *Vintage label*
- *1" foam or flat brushes (3)*
- *Acrylic paints, white and yellow*
- *Fine sandpaper*
- *Water-based stain*
- *Lint-free rag*
- *Acrylic sealer*

Step-by-Step Instructions

1. Using a 1" foam brush, apply two coats of white acrylic paint to the outer surface of the metal bucket. Allow to dry completely between coats.

2. Using a 1" foam brush, apply two coats of yellow acrylic paint to the inner surface of the metal bucket. Allow to dry completely between coats.

3. For a weathered or worn look, lightly sand the outside edges. Wipe clean. For an aged look, apply a small amount of water-based stain to the entire project after sanding, using a lint-free rag.

4. Adhere the vintage label to the center of the metal bucket.

5. Using a 1" foam brush, apply a thin coat of acrylic sealer to the entire inner and outer surfaces of the metal bucket, except on the label. Let dry.

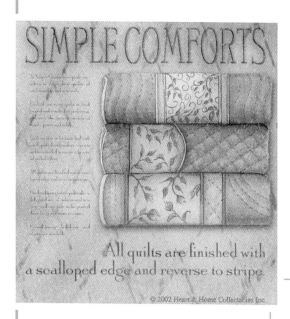

WASH DAY SCRAPBOOK PAGE

Materials

- *Scrapbook page*
- *Vintage label*
- *Wash-day-related photograph*
- *Decorative papers same size as scrapbook page, striped and solid*
- *Twine (13")*
- *Vintage clothespins (2)*
- *Infant T-shirt*
- *Glue or double-sided tape*

Step-by-Step Instructions

1. Adhere sheet of striped decorative paper to scrapbook page.
2. Create a title on the page by either handwriting the text on a sheet of solid decorative paper.
3. Optional: Use a computer to generate the text.
4. Adhere the title to the top-right corner of the scrapbook page.
5. Mount vintage label and photographs onto the solid decorative paper and arrange on the scrapbook page.
6. Create a clothesline with the twine and clothes pegs. Hang the infant T-shirt on the clothespins.
7. Glue the clothesline and infant T-shirt to the scrapbook page.
8. Optional: Add your own wash-day items to personalize the scrapbook page.

PAINTED LAUNDRY GIFT PAILS

Materials

- *Metal pails*
- *1" foam or flat brushes (2)*
- *Acrylic paint, assortment of colors including white and yellow*
- *Alphabet stencil or script paintbrush*
- *Stencils of laundry items*
- *Script paintbrush*
- *Pencil*
- *Acrylic sealer*
- *Gift items including soaps, towels, brushes, and spray bottles*

Step-by-Step Instructions

1. Using a 1" foam brush, apply two coats of acrylic paint to the entire surface of a pail. Choose a color to complement your gift item. Allow to dry completely between coats.
2. With pencil and alphabet stencil, trace text around the top of the pail. Refer to the color photograph on the opposite page for text or create your own personalized message.
3. Optional: Instead of using a stencil, you may freehand your own text.
4. Using a script paintbrush, fill in pencil marks with you choice of acrylic paint color. Let dry.
5. Paint laundry-related items onto the pail, using a stencil or freehand your own pictures.
6. Optional: If you do not want to paint an image onto the pail, you may to adhere a vintage label.
7. Using a 1" foam brush, apply a thin coat of acrylic sealer to the painted surface of the pail. Let dry.
8. Fill the painted pail with gift items.

LAUNDRY DAY PLAQUE

Materials

- 10"x5" piece of beadboard
- Vintage label
- 1" foam or flat brushes (2)
- Acrylic paint, white
- Fine sandpaper
- Water-based stain
- Lint-free rag
- Acrylic sealer
- Hammer
- 1" Decorative hooks or antique nails (5)
- Drill with $^1/_{16}$" drill bit
- Vintage clothespin
- 18-gauge wire (15")

Step-by-Step Instructions

1. Using a 1" foam brush, apply two coats of white acrylic paint to the beadboard. Allow to dry completely between coats.
2. For a weathered or worn look, lightly sand the outside edges. Wipe clean. For an aged look, apply a small amount of water-based stain to the entire project after sanding, using a lint-free rag.
3. Referring to the color photograph on the opposite page for placement, hammer in the decorative hooks or antique nails $^1/_4$" into the beadboard.
4. Adhere vintage label to the center of the beadboard.
5. Using a 1" foam brush, apply a thin coat of acrylic sealer to the beadboard, except on the label. Let dry.
6. Drill a hole through the top left and right corners of the beadboard and through the neck and tails of the clothespin.
7. Cut the 18-gauge wire in half. Working on one side at a time, feed one end of the wire through the back side of the beadboard. Feed the other end through the neck of the vintage clothespin. Twist ends in tight spirals to secure in place. Repeat this process for the opposite sides.

QUALITY SINCE 1840   GLENSBURG, OH

MACLAIN

© 2001 Heart & Home Collectables Inc.

LAUNDRY SOAP CONTAINERS

Materials

- Set of three round papier-mâché containers with lids
- Vintage labels (3)
- 1" foam or flat brushes (2)
- Acrylic paint, cream
- Fine sandpaper
- Water-based stain
- Lint-free rag
- Acrylic stain

Step-by-Step Instructions

1. Using a 1" foam brush, apply two coats of cream acrylic paint to the outer surface of each papier-mâché container, including the lid. Allow each coat to dry completely.
2. For a weathered or worn look, lightly sand the outside edges. Wipe clean. For an aged look, apply a small amount of water-based stain to the entire project after sanding, using a lint-free rag.
3. Adhere the vintage label to the center of each container.
4. Using a 1" foam brush, apply a thin coat of acrylic sealer to the exterior of each container and lid, except on the label. Let dry.

LAUNDRY ROOM CUPBOARD

Materials

- *8"x8"x4" wooden cupboard with door*
- *Vintage label*
- *1" foam or flat brushes (2)*
- *Acrylic paints, green and black*
- *Script paintbrush*
- *Fine sandpaper*
- *Water-based stain*
- *Lint-free rag*
- *Ruler*
- *Scissors*
- *8½"x11" decorative paper*
- *Spray adhesive*
- *Acrylic sealer*

Step-by-Step Instructions

1. Using a 1" foam, apply two coats of green acrylic paint to the entire surface of the wooden cupboard. Allow to dry completely between coats.
2. Using a script paintbrush and black acrylic paint, randomly add worn spots on edges only. Let dry.
3. For a weathered or worn look, lightly sand the outside edges. Wipe clean. For an aged look, apply a small amount of water-based stain to the entire project after sanding, using a lint-free rag.
4. Using ruler and scissors, measure and cut the decorative paper to the same dimension as the cupboard door.
5. Spray a thin coat of spray adhesive to the back side of the decorative paper and adhere to the front cupboard door.
6. Center and adhere the vintage label to the backboard of the wooden cupboard.
7. Using a 1" foam brush, apply a thin coat of acrylic sealer to the entire surface of the wooden cupboard, except on the decorative paper and label. Let dry.

VINTAGE SEWING BOX

Materials

- *Large vintage matchbox or a metal container with a hinged lid*
- *Vintage label*
- *Piece of balsa wood cut to the same measurements as the label*
- *1" foam or flat brush*
- *Acrylic paint, white*
- *Glue gun with clear glue sticks*
- *Assorted sewing notions*

Step-by-Step Instructions

1. Create a plaque by adhering the vintage label to the precut balsa wood.
2. Using the 1" foam brush, apply two coats of white acrylic paint to interior and exterior of the matchbox. Allow to dry completely between coats.
3. Glue the balsa wood plaque to the inside lid of the matchbox.
4. Fill with assorted sewing notions.

SEW PRECIOUS SCRAPBOOK PAGE

Materials

- *Scrapbook page*
- *Vintage labels (2)*
- *Photographs*
- *Decorative papers same size as scrapbook page, solid and plaid*
- *Glue or double-sided tape*
- *Black felt fabric*
- *Sewing needle*
- *Double-sided tape*
- *3"x3" lace doily*
- *Cardstock*
- *Sewing notions including buttons, snap fasteners, old needle package, and 15" piece of cloth tape measure*

Step-by-Step Instructions

1. Cut and adhere the decorative paper onto the scrapbook page, giving the page a "patchwork" appearance.
2. Create a title on the page by handwriting the text on a sheet of solid decorative paper.
3. Optional: Use a computer to generate the text.
4. Attach the title to a piece of black felt fabric using a sewing needle. Adhere the fabric to the page.
5. Adhere the lace doily to the scrapbook page.
6. Prepare all mats for labels and photographs by measuring cardstock the size of each and adding $1/4$". Either cut or rip the measured cardstock and adhere the labels and photographs onto each piece.
7. Optional: For our pictures we have doubled matted using black textured fabric, then added a cream background, again cutting $1/4$" larger for the border.
8. Arrange and adhere matted photographs and labels onto scrapbook page.
9. Decorate with sewing notions.

Chapter Five

A PRETTY FEMININE TOUCH

LAUREN'S
IMPORTED
BRIDAL
DRESSES
Haute Couture
© 2002 Heart & Home Collectables Inc.

FEATHERS
FINE LINENS

Sure to compliment any decor.

Ornately carved furnishings by local artisans

Abbey Lane

Fine Furniture

© 2002 Heart & Home Collectables Inc.

WILDFLOWERS

© 2001 Heart & Home Collectables Inc.

CAMELLIA

BATH   SOAP

CAMELLIA
BATH
SOAP
4 oz.

Fragrant as flowers after the rain.

© 2002 Heart & Home Collectables Inc.

VENETIAN ✦ VANITY

Venetian Vanity

A Bath and Boidoir Company

© 2002 Heart & Home Collectables Inc.

PINK BOUTIQUE PLAQUE

Materials

- *9¹/₂"x6³/₄" wooden plaque*
- *Vintage label*
- *Fine sandpaper*
- *1" foam or flat brushes (2)*
- *¹/₃" flat paintbrush*
- *Acrylic paint, white*
- *Ruler*
- *Pencil*
- *8¹/₂"x11" decorative paper*
- *Scissors*
- *Spray adhesive*
- *Hammer*
- *1" decorative or antique nails (3)*
- *Water-based stain*
- *Lint-free rag*
- *Acrylic sealer*
- *Sheer ribbon (25")*
- *Heavy-duty stapler*

Step-by-Step Instructions

1. Lightly sand the entire surface of the wooden plaque, removing any rough edges. Wipe clean.
2. Using a 1" foam brush, apply two coats of white acrylic paint to the front of the wooden plaque. Allow to dry completely between coats.
3. Using a ruler and pencil, measure and mark a 8¹/₂"x5³/₄" rectangle on your decorative paper. Cut out with scissors.
4. Apply a thin coat of spray adhesive to the back side of the decorative paper and carefully position it on the front of the wooden plaque. Smooth out any ridges.
5. Adhere the vintage label to the center of the plaque.
6. Referring to the color photograph on the opposite page, hammer the decorative nails ¹/₄" deep into the front of the wooden plaque.
7. Using a ¹/₃" flat paintbrush, apply a thin coat of white acrylic paint to the decorative nails. Let dry.
8. For a weathered or worn look, lightly sand the outside edges of the plaque. Wipe clean. For an aged look, apply a small amount of water-based stain to the entire project after sanding, using a lint-free rag.
9. Using a 1" foam brush, apply a thin coat of acrylic sealer to the plaque edges only.
10. Create a center bow with the sheer ribbon and staple the tails of the bow to the top left and right corners on the back side of the wooden plaque.

HAND-PAINTED TALC CONTAINER

Materials

- *Papier-mâché talc container*
- *1" foam or flat brushes (2)*
- *Acrylic paints, assortment including cream and white*
- *1/4" flat paintbrush*
- *Paintbrushes, assortment including flat, shading, and script*
- *Circle or oval template*
- *Graphite paper*
- *Pencil*
- *Floral Designs pattern #1 or #2 on page 125*
- *Alphabet stencil*
- *Acrylic sealer*

Step-by-Step Instructions

1. Using a 1" foam brush, apply two coats of cream acrylic paint to the entire surface of the papier-mâché talc container. Allow to dry completely between coats.
2. Using a 1/4" flat paintbrush, apply one coat of white acrylic paint to the top section, raised edges, and lid of the container. Let dry.
3. Using the circle template, trace a circle on the front of the container. Fill in the circle with white acrylic paint. Let dry.
4. Using graphite paper and a pencil, transfer a Floral Designs pattern onto the circle.
5. Using an assortment of paintbrushes and acrylic paints, paint in the floral patterns. Let dry.
6. Referring to the above colored photograph, add the text, using an alphabet stencil.
7. Using a 1" foam brush, apply a thin coat of acrylic sealer to the entire outer surface. Let dry.

ORGANZA GIFT BAG

Materials

- *6"x8" organza bag*
- *Vintage label with an adhesive backing*
- *Decorative cord (17")*
- *Scented bath salt*

Step-by-Step Instructions

1. Lay the organza bag on a flat surface, smooth out any bumps or ridges.
2. Apply the vintage label to the front of the bag.
3. Carefully fill the organza bag with scented bath salt.
4. Tie the top of the bag, using the decorative cord.

DISPLAY HAT BOX

Rose's HATS and Accessories

Materials

- *9¹/₂"x5" papier-mâché hat box*
- *Vintage label*
- *1" foam or flat brushes (3)*
- *Acrylic paints, antique white and yellow*
- *Ruler*
- *Pencil with eraser*
- *Drill with a ¹/₁₆" drill bit*
- *30" decorative cord*
- *⁵/₁₆" grommet*
- *25" double-ended tassel with cord*
- *Acrylic sealer*
- *Glue gun with clear glue stick*

Step-by-Step Instructions

1. Using a 1" foam brush, apply two coats of antique white acrylic paint to the entire outer surface of the papier-mâché hat box and the lid. Allow to dry completely between coats.
2. Using a ruler and pencil, mark 1" vertical stripes around the entire outer surface of the base of the hat box.
3. Using a 1" foam brush, fill in every other stripe with yellow acrylic paint. Let dry. Erase any exposed pencil marks.
4. Place the lid on the box and adhere the vintage label to front side of the hat box.
5. Using a glue gun, add the decorative cord around the bottom edge of the lid. Cut off excess.
6. Using a 1" foam brush, apply a thin coat of acrylic sealer to the entire outer surface, except on the label. Let dry.
7. Drill a hole in the top center of the lid. Insert grommet and secure in place.
8. Feed the cord of the double-ended tassel through the grommet and tie a knot to secure.

BRIDAL KEEPSAKE BOX

Materials

- *11"x3"x3½" papier-mâché box*
- *Vintage label*
- *1" foam or flat brushes (2)*
- *Acrylic paint, dark sage green*
- *Ruler*
- *Scissors*
- *8½"x11" decorative paper*
- *Spray adhesive*
- *Fine sandpaper*
- *Water-based stain*
- *Lint-free rag*
- *Acrylic sealer*

Step-by-Step Instructions

1. Using a 1" foam brush, apply two coats of dark sage green acrylic paint to the entire outer surface of the base of the papier-mâché box. Allow to dry completely between coats.
2. Using a ruler and scissors, measure and cut decorative paper to fit the lid. Apply a thin coat of spray adhesive to the back side of the piece of paper and carefully apply it to the lid.
3. For a weathered or worn look, lightly sand the outside edges. Wipe clean. For an aged look, apply a small amount of water-based stain to the entire project after sanding, using a lint-free rag.
4. Adhere the vintage label to the front side of the box.
5. Using a 1" foam brush, apply a thin coat of acrylic sealer to the painted surface of the box, except on the label. Let dry.

WOODEN BRIDAL BOX

Materials

- *6¹/₂"x5"x3¹/₄" decorative wooden box with hinged lid*
- *Vintage labels (2)*
- *Scissors*
- *Pencil*
- *1" foam or flat brushes (2)*
- *Acrylic paint, white*
- *Fine sandpaper*
- *Water-based stain*
- *Lint-free rag*
- *Acrylic sealer*

Step-by-Step Instructions

1. Using a 1" foam brush, apply two coats of white acrylic paint over the outer and inner surfaces of the wooden box. Allow to dry completely between coats.
2. For a weathered or worn look, lightly sand the outside edges. Wipe clean. For an aged look, apply a small amount of water-based stain to the entire project after sanding, using a lint-free rag.
3. Center and adhere one vintage label to the top of the lid.
4. Using a 1" foam brush, apply a thin coat of acrylic sealer to the entire outer and inner surfaces of the wooden box, except on the label.
5. Cut remaining vintage labels to fit inside the box, centering each motif within a box "window."
6. Adhere each motif in place.

BRIDAL SLIDING BOX AND CUPS

Materials

- 7³⁄₄"x3¹⁄₂"x3³⁄₄" wooden box with sliding lid
- Vintage labels (3)
- 1" foam or flat brushes (2)
- Acrylic paint, white
- Scissors
- Enamel cups (2)
- Fine sandpaper
- Water-based stain
- Lint-free rag
- Acrylic sealer

Step-by-Step Instructions

1. Cut two of the labels vertically between the image and text. Discard the portion of the labels with the text.
2. Adhere one cut label to the front side of each enamel cup.
3. Using a 1" foam brush, apply two coats of white acrylic paint to the entire surface of the wooden box. Allow to dry completely between coats.
4. For a weathered or worn look, lightly sand the outside edges. Wipe clean. For an aged look, apply a small amount of water-based stain to the entire project after sanding, using a lint-free rag.
5. Center and adhere the third vintage label to the sliding lid.
6. Using a 1" foam brush, apply a thin coat of acrylic sealer to the entire surface of the wooden box, except on the label.

DOUBLE-HANDLED KEEPSAKE BOX

Materials

- 6"x6"x3" papier-mâché box with lid
- Vintage label
- 1" foam or flat brushes (3)
- Acrylic paints, cream and pale green
- 2¾" wooden handles (2)
- ⅛" or ¼" angular paintbrush
- Script paintbrush
- Fine sandpaper
- Water-based stain
- Lint-free rag
- Stylus
- 18-gauge wire (10")
- Needle-nosed pliers

Step-by-Step Instructions

1. Using a 1" foam brush, apply two coats of cream acrylic paint to the entire outer surface of the papier-mâché box and the lid. Allow to dry completely between coats.
2. Using a 1" foam brush, apply two coats of cream acrylic paint to both wooden handles. Allow to dry completely between coats.
3. Using pale green acrylic paint, freehand random vine design, using ⅛" angular paintbrush for leaves and script paintbrush for vines.
4. Optional: Stencil a small pattern on top of the lid. Let dry.
5. For a weathered or worn look, lightly sand the outside edges. Wipe clean. For an aged look, apply a small amount of water-based stain to the entire project after sanding, using a lint-free rag.
6. Using a stylus, pierce two holes on one side of the lid, 2¾" apart, for the wooden handles. Repeat on opposite side.
7. Feed 18-gauge wire through each wooden handle. Attach the handles to the sides of the box by feeding each end of the wire through the holes. Secure tightly on the inside by twisting the wire in a spiral with the needle-nosed pliers.
8. Adhere the vintage label to the center of the lid.

How to Live on 24 Hours a Day

CHRISTINA'S
FINE CHINA

FEATHERS
FINE LINENS

Sure to complement any décor

FINE CHINA BOX

Materials

- *Papier-mâché box with lid*
- *Vintage label*
- *1" foam or flat brush*
- *Acrylic paints, navy blue and white*
- *Script paintbrush*
- *Fine sandpaper*
- *Water-based stain*
- *Lint-free rag*
- *Decorative fabric*
- *Glue gun with clear glue sticks*
- *¹/₂"-thick decorative cord*
- *Decorative tassels (2)*

Step-by-Step Instructions

1. Using a 1" foam brush, apply two coats of navy blue acrylic paint to the entire surface of the papier-mâché box. Allow to dry completely between coats.
2. Using a script paintbrush and white acrylic paint, freehand a random vine design on the lid and base of the box. Let dry.
3. For a weathered or worn look, lightly sand the outside edges. Wipe clean. For an aged look, apply a small amount of water-based stain to the entire project after sanding, using a lint-free rag.
4. Line the base of the box with decorative fabric. Hot-glue securely into place.
5. Referring to the above colored photograph for placement, hot-glue the decorative cord and tassels to the base of the box.
6. Adhere the vintage label to the center of the lid.

DECORATIVE STORAGE BOX

Materials

- Large papier-mâché box with lid
- Vintage label
- 1" foam or flat brush
- Acrylic paints, white and light blue
- Script paintbrush
- Acrylic sealer

Step-by-Step Instructions

1. Using a 1" foam brush, apply two coats of light blue acrylic paint to the papier-mâché box, including the lid. Allow to dry completely between coats.
2. Using white acrylic paint, freehand a random vine design on the box. Let dry.
3. Optional: Using a ruler and pencil, mark 1" or 1½" vertical stripes around the entire surface of the base of the medium box. Fill in every other stripe with the white acrylic paint. Let dry.
4. Adhere the vintage label to the front side of the box.
5. Apply a thin coat of acrylic sealer to the entire outer surface of the box and lid, except on the label. Let dry.

WINE GIFT BOX

Materials

- *Papier-mâché cylinder with lid*
- *Vintage label*
- *1" foam or flat brushes (3)*
- *Acrylic paints, cream and celery green*
- *Ruler*
- *Pencil*
- *¼" flat paintbrush*
- *Acrylic stain*
- *Soft clothes (2)*

Step-by-Step Instructions

1. Using a 1" foam brush, apply two coats of cream acrylic paint to the outer surface of the cylinder. Allow to dry completely between coats.
2. Using a 1" foam brush, apply two coats of celery green acrylic paint to the outer surface of the cylinder's lid. Allow to dry completely between coats.
3. Using a ruler and pencil, measure and mark ¼" lines from the top of the cylinder to the bottom, creating a thin striped pattern around the entire outer surface.
4. Using the ¼" flat paintbrush, apply one coat of celery green acrylic paint to every other stripe. Allow to dry completely.
5. Center and adhere the vintage label to the front side of the cylinder.
6. Using the soft cloth, apply stain to the entire painted surface for the box and lid, except on the label. Wipe off excess and allow to dry completely.

GARDEN TOOL TRAY

Materials

- 9"x10" wooden tray
- Vintage labels (6)
- 1" foam or flat brushes (2)
- Acrylic paint, white
- Fine sandpaper
- Water-based stain
- Lint-free rag
- Acrylic sealer

Step-by-Step Instructions

1. Using a 1" foam brush, apply two coats of white acrylic paint to the entire surface of the wooden tray. Allow to dry completely between coats.
2. Working with one vintage label at a time, randomly adhere them to the inner base of the tray.
3. For a weathered or worn look, lightly sand the outside edges. Wipe clean. For an aged look, apply a small amount of water-based stain to the entire project after sanding, using a lint-free rag.
4. Using a 1" foam brush, apply a thin coat of acrylic sealer to the entire tray. Let dry.

PAINTED GARDEN PAIL

Materials

- *7"x 7" metal bucket*
- *Vintage label*
- *1" foam or flat brushes (4)*
- *Crackle medium*
- *Acrylic paints, lavender, white, and moss green*
- *¼" angular paintbrush*
- *Fine sandpaper*
- *Water-based stain*
- *Lint-free rag*
- *Acrylic sealer*

Step-by-Step Instructions

1. Using a 1" foam brush, apply two coats of lavender acrylic paint to the entire surface of the metal bucket. Allow to dry completely between coats.
2. Using a 1" foam brush, brush one coat of crackle medium horizontally on the outside of the metal bucket. Follow instructions on bottle.
3. Using a 1" foam brush, brush one coat of white acrylic paint horizontally on the outside of the metal bucket. Let dry.
4. Using a ¼" angular paintbrush, apply moss green acrylic paint to highlight sections of the bottom and top edges. Let dry.
5. Center and adhere the vintage label to the front side of the metal bucket.
6. For a weathered or worn look, lightly sand the outside edges. Wipe clean. For an aged look, apply a small amount of water-based stain to the entire project after sanding, using a lint-free rag.
7. Using a 1" foam brush, apply a thin coat of acrylic sealer to the entire surface of the metal bucket, except on the label. Let dry.

RIVERVIEW GARDEN CENTER

We fulfill your gardening needs for every season.

© 2002 Heart & Home Collectables Inc.

PAPIER-MÂCHÉ GARDEN BOOK

Materials

- *Papier-mâché book*
- *1″ foam or flat brushes (3)*
- *Acrylic paints, assortment of colors including white and yellow*
- *¼″ flat paintbrush*
- *Paintbrushes, assortment including flat, shading, and script*
- *Ruler*
- *Pencil*
- *Circle template*
- *Graphite paper*
- *Floral Designs pattern #1 or #2 on page 125*
- *Gray pencil crayon*
- *Fine sandpaper*
- *Water-based stain*
- *Lint-free rag*
- *Acrylic sealer*

Step-by-Step Instructions

1. Using a 1″ foam brush, apply two coats of white acrylic paint to the outer surface of the papier-mâché book. Allow to dry completely between coats.
2. Using a ruler and pencil, mark the front cover edges to form a border.
3. Using a 1″ foam brush, fill in with two coats of yellow acrylic. Allow to dry completely between coats.
4. Trace a circle on the front cover of the book, using a circle template.
5. Using ¼″ flat paintbrush, fill in the circle with white acrylic paint. Let dry.
6. Using graphite paper and a pencil, transfer a Floral Designs pattern onto the circle.
7. Optional: Instead of using the provided pattern, you can freehand your own floral design.
8. Using the assortment of paintbrushes and acrylic paints, fill in the floral pattern and add shading. Let dry.
9. Referring to the color photograph on the opposite page, and using a gray pencil crayon, write the appropriate text.
10. For a weathered or worn look, lightly sand the outside edges. Wipe clean. For an aged look, apply a small amount of water-based stain to the entire project after sanding, using a lint-free rag.
11. Using a 1″ foam brush, apply a thin coat of acrylic sealer to the entire outer surface of the book. Let dry.

DECORATIVE
BABY SHIRT
(INSTRUCTIONS ON PAGE 14)

Enlarge or reduce to desired size.

DECORATIVE SNOWMEN FACES

(INSTRUCTIONS ON PAGE 60)

FACE #1

FACE #2

Enlarge or reduce to desired size.

SNOWMEN WINDOW FRAME PLACEMENT

(INSTRUCTIONS ON PAGE 63)

SNOWMAN
#1

SNOWMAN
#2

SNOWMAN
#3

SNOWMAN
#4

SNOWMEN WINDOW FRAME #1

Enlarge or reduce to desired size.

SNOWMEN WINDOW FRAME #2

Enlarge or reduce to desired size.

SNOWMEN
WINDOW FRAME
#3

Enlarge or reduce to desired size.

SNOWMEN WINDOW FRAME #4

Enlarge or reduce to desired size.

FLORAL DESIGNS
(INSTRUCTIONS ON PAGE 98 AND 116)

FLORAL #1

FLORAL #2

Enlarge or reduce to desired size.

LABEL INVENTORY

The labels featured in this book are from Heart & Home's unique Melissa Frances™ peel-and-stick labels.

Most of the project materials are available online at **www.melissafrances.com** or at your local craft store.

METRIC EQUIVALENCY CHARTS

mm-millimeters cm-centimeters
inches to millimeters and centimeters

inches	mm	cm	inches	cm	inches	cm
⅛	3	0.3	9	22.9	30	76.2
¼	6	0.6	10	25.4	31	78.7
½	13	1.3	12	30.5	33	83.8
⅝	16	1.6	13	33.0	34	86.4
¾	19	1.9	14	35.6	35	88.9
⅞	22	2.2	15	38.1	36	91.4
1	25	2.5	16	40.6	37	94.0
1¼	32	3.2	17	43.2	38	96.5
1½	38	3.8	18	45.7	39	99.1
1¾	44	4.4	19	48.3	40	101.6
2	51	5.1	20	50.8	41	104.1
2½	64	6.4	21	53.3	42	106.7
3	76	7.6	22	55.9	43	109.2
3½	89	8.9	23	58.4	44	111.8
4	102	10.2	24	61.0	45	114.3
4½	114	11.4	25	63.5	46	116.8
5	127	12.7	26	66.0	47	119.4
6	152	15.2	27	68.6	48	121.9
7	178	17.8	28	71.1	49	124.5
8	203	20.3	29	73.7	50	127.0

yards to meters

yards	meters	yards	meters	yards	meters	yards	meters	yards	meters
⅛	0.11	2⅛	1.94	4⅛	3.77	6⅛	5.60	8⅛	7.43
¼	0.23	2¼	2.06	4¼	3.89	6¼	5.72	8¼	7.54
⅜	0.34	2⅜	2.17	4⅜	4.00	6⅜	5.83	8⅜	7.66
½	0.46	2½	2.29	4½	4.11	6½	5.94	8½	7.77
⅝	0.57	2⅝	2.40	4⅝	4.23	6⅝	6.06	8⅝	7.89
¾	0.69	2¾	2.51	4¾	4.34	6¾	6.17	8¾	8.00
⅞	0.80	2⅞	2.63	4⅞	4.46	6⅞	6.29	8⅞	8.12
1	0.91	3	2.74	5	4.57	7	6.40	9	8.23
1⅛	1.03	3⅛	2.86	5⅛	4.69	7⅛	6.52	9⅛	8.34
1¼	1.14	3¼	2.97	5¼	4.80	7¼	6.63	9¼	8.46
1⅜	1.26	3⅜	3.09	5⅜	4.91	7⅜	6.74	9⅜	8.57
1½	1.37	3½	3.20	5½	5.03	7½	6.86	9½	8.69
1⅝	1.49	3⅝	3.31	5⅝	5.14	7⅝	6.97	9⅝	8.80
1¾	1.60	3¾	3.43	5¾	5.26	7¾	7.09	9¾	8.92
1⅞	1.71	3⅞	3.54	5⅞	5.37	7⅞	7.20	9⅞	9.03
2	1.83	4	3.66	6	5.49	8	7.32	10	9.14

INDEX